Antonia Aline Rodrigues
Jaqueline Silva da Rosa

Difficulties in the job market for secretarial professionals

Antonia Aline Rodrigues
Jaqueline Silva da Rosa

Difficulties in the job market for secretarial professionals

ScienciaScripts

Imprint

Cover image: www.ingimage.com

This book is a translation from the original published under ISBN 978-3-330-76878-9.

Publisher:
Sciencia Scripts
is a trademark of
Dodo Books Indian Ocean Ltd. and OmniScriptum S.R.L publishing group

120 High Road, East Finchley, London, N2 9ED, United Kingdom
Str. Armeneasca 28/1, office 1, Chisinau MD-2012, Republic of Moldova, Europe
Managing Directors: Ieva Konstantinova, Victoria Ursu
info@omniscriptum.com

Printed at: see last page
ISBN: 978-620-8-60055-6

SUMMARY

I dedicate this work to God for having given me strength and courage during this journey, helping me to face all the obstacles and for having given me a wonderful family who have been with me from the start and whose encouragement and understanding have been fundamental in this journey.

ACKNOWLEDGMENTS

In concluding this dream, I would first of all like to thank God, the main person responsible for all of this, for allowing me to successfully reach this stage in my life.

I would like to thank my family, my mother Socorro, my brother Pedro and my sister-in-law Tâmara, to whom I owe part of what I have and what I am, for their dedication, support, encouragement and love, for always believing in me and giving me the chance to make my dreams come true.

To my advisor Prof. MSc. Jaqueline Silva da Rosa, for accepting my project, for her safe and competent guidance, her constant encouragement, her patience and her dedication, her contributions were significant for my intellectual and personal growth and this helped me to complete my monograph.

To all the professors in the Executive Secretarial Department at UFRR, who shared their knowledge in a special way.

Finally, to the friends and colleagues who helped directly or indirectly to achieve another stage in my life, and who shared many of my joys and sorrows and helped me in my academic training.

The Federal University of Roraima, for allowing me to study and complete the Executive Secretarial course.

Thank you to everyone who, in one way or another, helped me reach this moment.

Let your efforts defy impossibilities - remember that the great things of man have been achieved from what seemed impossible.

(Charles Chaplin).

SUMMARY

Due to the highly competitive nature of the job market, executive secretaries have to keep up with the changes taking place. The general aim of this study is to verify the difficulties encountered by Executive Secretarial (ES) professionals in entering the job market. To this end, a qualitative study was carried out, with in-depth interviews with Executive Secretarial professionals and Human Resources managers. After analyzing the data, it was found that the difficulties faced by ES professionals in entering the job market are: a lack of vacancies for ES in public tenders; a shortage of vacancies in the private sector; a lack of adequate remuneration for the profession; a lack of recognition from managers; a lack of knowledge of their duties; and a demanding, competitive market.

Key words: Executive Secretary. Job market. Employability.

1 INTRODUCTION

The competitive market demands that professionals have, in addition to technical and specific knowledge, behavioral skills that promote comprehensive training with a constant search for updating to keep up with the changes proposed by the market. As a result of this high level of competitiveness, in order to improve their employability, Executive Secretaries (ES) must keep up with the changes and adapt their profile to the demands of the job market. According to Veiga (2007), the professional who only carried out orders has given way to a professional who is aware of the great importance of the position within organizations. Responsibilities have increased and with this has come the need to improve oneself in order to keep up with the company's changes.

The integration of professionals into the job market is linked to the training and perception they must have in order to see the opportunities presented by organizations, increasing their chances of employability. This, in turn, is and will increasingly be a determining factor in the employment and permanence of all professionals, including executive secretaries.

According to Saviani (1997), a high employability rate depends on factors such as creativity, empathy, flexibility, extroversion, common sense, leadership, initiative, emotional intelligence and global culture. It can be seen that these factors go beyond the technical skills improved in the qualification of professionals. Against this backdrop, in which professionals are seeking employability, secretarial professionals must develop technical and human skills in order to keep up with the pace of change and grow and improve in order to stand out in the job market. In the meantime, we felt the need to find out what difficulties exist in the job market for executive secretarial professionals, based on their perceptions.

Creativity, innovation, initiative and leadership are some of the various buzzwords used in the context of organizations. In this sense, the subject of competence is being discussed more and more, both on an individual level (MCCLELLAND, 1973; ZARIFIAN, 1996; LE BOTERF, 2001; FLEURY; FLEURY, 2001 apud FLEURY; SARSUR, 2007) or in the Collective dimension (LEONARD-BARTON, 1992; NORDH AUG; GRONH AU G, 1994; RUAS, 2000; BECKER, 2004; WEICK, 1993; WEICK; ROBERTS, 1993; SANDBERG, 1996; ZARIFIAN, 2001; LÊ BOTERF, 2003 and BOREHAM, 2004 apud ROSA, 2007).

This discussion about competencies directly and proportionally supports employability. Contemporary professionals must excel in behavioral aspects, not just in technical skills. In this sense, understanding and diagnosing the difficulties encountered by executive secretarial professionals in entering the job market can go some way to evaluating opportunities, anticipating scenarios and, above all, pointing out some directions for professionals in the field.

Understanding the reality from the point of view of the executive secretarial professionals themselves helps us to think and rethink their practices and, above all, to reflect on their own qualifications as professionals. Given this context, the driving force behind this research is to verify the difficulties faced by Executive Secretarial professionals in entering the job market. To this end, this work is structured in 5 chapters, the first of which is the Introduction, which presents the research topic, the objectives and the justification. Chapter 2 presents the Theoretical Framework, which includes topics such as the Labor Market, Employability: the challenge for professionals, Factors that maintain employability and Executive Secretarial Professionals and their Competencies; Chapter 3 presents the methodology, which presents the classification of the research, data collection and analysis techniques. Chapter 4 presents and analyzes the data. Finally, there are the Final Considerations, followed by the References and Appendix.

1.1 Research Problem

What are the difficulties encountered by executive secretarial professionals in entering the job market?

1.2 Objectives

1.2.1General Objective

To verify the difficulties encountered by executive secretarial professionals in finding their place in the job market.

1.2.2Specific Objectives

a. To identify the socio-demographic profile of executive secretarial professionals

b. List the main difficulties encountered by SE professionals in entering the job market.

c. To describe the profile of SE professionals that the job market wants, based on the perceptions of Human Resources managers.

1.3 Justification

In order to stay in the job market, professionals need to have in-depth knowledge of their field of work, as well as the skills required for the position they will be given and maintain their competitive edge. People live in an era of constant change amid increased competition and globalized competition.

According to Natalense (1988), the role of the Executive Secretary has undergone these transformations to meet the demands brought about by globalization and must be qualified to act and exercise his professional role in the most diverse companies or institutions, acting as: Executive Advisor, Manager, Entrepreneur and Consuitor able to exercise competent management.

This professional must find in the company the conditions and environment for learning and developing their skills, meeting the expectations of the organization and their own. Given this context, the driving force behind this study is to assess the difficulties encountered by executive secretarial professionals in entering the job market. Investigating this topic provides professionals with knowledge and broadens their perception of employability, since they can reflect on and assess the difficulties of entering the job market. It also provides data on the profile of the SE professional that the market wants and which should be reflected in educational institutions.

2 THEORETICAL FRAMEWORK

2.1 Job market

According to Bertolino (2002), the work environment is competitive and selective for professionals, meaning that an organization's growth and results are achieved at the expense of personal skills, not just technical skills. As a result, society is looking for professionals who are involved with the whole and concerned with satisfactory results for the organization.

Increased competition and globalized competition is a notable reality in the world of work. Working relationships have been completely innovated by globalization, making the role assigned to each professional within organizations more complex (FACHINI, 2009).

In this sense, Arruda (2010) points out that in the job market, knowledge is one of the fundamental skills for professionals at all levels to achieve their growth objectives, such as getting a promotion or even a new opportunity in the world of work.

Garcia and D'Elia (2005) present a table of changing market demands. See table 1 below:

Chart 1: Profile of the professional in general.

The 70s	The 80s	The 90s	21st century
Experience is a tool used in command	Education is your command tool	Your performance is your command tool	The professional and his team are the tools for his success and that of others.
Accommodated	Confident	Curious	Scholar
Dependent	Politics	Independent	You have a global view of things
Resists change	Adjust to change	Generate Change	Leading change

Looking for a Freight Forwarder	Try to be cooperative	Try to be a facilitator	Try to be Creative
Your salary is determined by the company	Your salary is negotiated by the company	Your salary is earned by the importance of your work	Your results are achieved through the hard work of you and your team
His recognition is the result of his professional experience.	Their knowledge is based on academic theory	Your knowledge is the fruit of the practical application of theory	Your knowledge is the fruit of continuous learning

Source: Garcia and D'Elia (200,5 p.24).

Table 1 shows the evolution that the job market requires and it is clear that, over time, professionals have been moving away from a more rigid posture and towards a more flexible posture centered on knowledge and the search for it. According to D'elia (1997), the job market is looking for professionals who are awakened to a new context and who therefore stand out from the rest.

Professionals need to be able to cope with the demands of the competitive job market, especially in terms of specific knowledge related to their profession. However, as Minarelli (1995) states, it is not enough for a person to have a certain professional qualification, because the market demands that they stand out, that they have a difference and that they are employable.

According to Veiga (2007), the professional who carried out orders has given way to a new professional who is aware of the value of the position within companies. Responsibilities have increased and, as a result, there is a need to improve in order to keep up with transformations. In the face of current market competition, professionals must adapt to these demands, building a profile that the job market wants, becoming a professional with multiple skills and competencies combined with characteristics such as training, ethics, knowledge and the ability to adjust to different changes, making them employable professionals. See table 2 below:

Table 2: Basic Employability Ratio

I What companies need:

• Knowledge
• Skills
• Durable skills
• Troubleshooting
• Innovation
• Creativity
• Added value
• Flexibility
• Motivation and commitment

Source: Adapted from Chiavenato (2002, p. 87).

Companies want more than technical skills, they want human and conceptual skills[1] . These skills must be developed and improved so that professionals can be better placed in the job market and, consequently, more employable. In this sense, with regard to the job market,

1 Human Skills "encompasses an understanding of people and their needs, interests and attitudes. The ability to [...] work with people". Conceptual Ability "involves the ability to understand and deal with the complexity of the whole organization and to use intellect to formulate strategies". Creativity, planning, abstract reasoning and understanding the context of situations are manifestations of conceptual ability (MAXIMIANO, 2004, p.66).

Chiavenato (2002, p.40) points out that it is made up of "companies and the job opportunities they offer. The greater the number of companies in a given region, the greater the labor market and its potential for vacancies and job opportunities".

Companies are looking for professionals who add value to the organization. In a highly competitive market, they choose the best candidates to join the workforce, those professionals who have skills and competencies such as: qualifications, creativity, innovation, flexibility and the ability to work in a team. The obstacle is not just being able to enter the job market, but ensuring employability, i.e. being an employable professional.

2.2 Employability: the challenge for professionals

Employability is a term that is currently being debated and can be understood as the actions taken by people to develop skills and seek knowledge in order to get a job in the labor market, whether formal or informal. Through it, it is possible to become the manager of your own career, being responsible for your gains and losses (NASCIMENTO et al., 2005).

According to Carvalho (2002), employability is understood to mean any professional who has employable qualities, thus representing a dynamic concept concerning the world of work in which it expresses everything the individual must have for their profound and indispensable ability to adapt and fit into this globalized market.

Hilsdorf (2008) states that employability is a dynamic issue and the list of prerequisites needed to be desired by the job market is constantly growing and the essential skills are becoming more extensive as time goes by. This situation forces professionals to build on, present and expand the knowledge they generate during their professional career. Knowledge in this field is the main and essential ally for professionals: they have to learn continuously. Peres (2005) states that professionals in the 21st century need to have authentic training in what they are prepared to work or perform, as well as a general education. It can be seen that there are aspects that are included, or rather, help employability to be sustainable.

Employability today is one of the biggest challenges for people. The globalization of the economy, the scenario of changes and transformations, the winds of competitiveness and the intense productivity and quality programs are changing the role of professionals in companies. And, in turn, they are profoundly altering the professional profile of employees. Anyone who doesn't fit this new profile is bound to lose their job to someone else who is better suited to the new demands and expectations of the market. A true natural selection of professionals, which is called employability (CHIAVENATO, 2002, p.86).

Minarelli (1995) states that professionals need to recycle themselves periodically so that they can keep their knowledge up to date and develop the skills to face the changes in the job market. To increase their employability and develop their careers by building their own foundations. Chiavenato (2002) corroborates the above author and asserts that in the competitive world in which we live, it is increasingly important to develop employability by preparing yourself adequately to maintain your professionalism, as well as developing and improving your career performance, since qualification must be a permanent concern for this professional.

Faced with this new reality, professionals need to add value to themselves in order to become employable. Attitudes such as proactivity, commitment, creativity and flexibility make a difference in the job market. And, with all these requirements, in order to be employable, professionals must constantly seek qualification, following prior career preparation and developing the skills and knowledge needed in the different areas of the job market. However, it can happen that professionals are insecure about their employability, which includes factors such as: competencies, skills, behaviors and knowledge appropriate to their job profile.

2.1.1Factors for maintaining employability

The frequent changes in the job market and in society in general require professionals to have an enormous capacity to adapt to the evolving demands of the job market in the world of professions. Baggio et al. (2005) point to four factors considered essential to maintaining employability levels today: adapting to change, a profile suited to the profession, networking and continuing education.

Chiavenato (2002) indicates some attitudes that can improve a professional's employability in the job market: *a)* evaluate and diversify your professional activities; *b)* improve and expand your communication skills - don't stand still; *c)* constantly recycle yourself ; *d)* treat your career as if it were a real business; *e)* do your own personal marketing; *f)* develop your network of social relationships: your *networking;* don't think of yourself as a mere employee; *g)* Learn to deal with people and add mobility and multifunctionality. These attitudes enable professionals to develop the knowledge, skills and competence to succeed in their professional careers.

In fact, the reality of the world of work is changing, and this is partly due to market demands and changes in professional profiles. These, in turn, must adapt to these changes. And for skilled and visionary professionals, it is recommended that they become agents of change, extracting from these their main competitive advantages .[2]

Some skills are fundamental for professionals who want to succeed in changing environments: adaptation and flexibility to new scenarios, a vision of the future, good interpersonal relationships and self-confidence in their qualifications, guaranteeing these professionals better conditions for adapting to transformations and enjoying their benefits,

---

2 See Porter (1989).

softening the impact of their weaknesses and some difficulties (BAGGIO et al. , 2005). See Table 3 below:

Box 3: The foundations of employability

Always evolving	Gaining a competitive edge	Contributing value	Meeting objectives and being indispensable	Being reliable	Being action-oriented: making it happen
Learning to learn	Developing skills and competencies	Adding value	Being responsible	Being loyal	Have personal initiative and a sense of entrepreneurship
The basics of employability					

Source: Adapted from Chiavenato (2002, p. 91).

According to Minarelli (1995), the six pillars that support employability are: vocational suitability, professional competence, suitability, physical and mental health, financial reserve and alternative sources and relationships. The combination of all of these gives the professional security and employability, i.e. the ability to generate work, to work and to earn. These pillars need to be connected and articulated with each other. The articulation between these aspects generates the synergy necessary for employability.

The frequent changes taking place in the workplace and in society in general require professionals to have an enormous capacity to adapt. Attributing these factors to maintaining employability establishes the professional's ability to overcome the current competitiveness and is essential for maintaining employability.

2.4 Executive Secretary Professionals and their Competencies

We live in a world of constant change which requires professionals to keep up to date in order to meet the needs of the market (MINARELLI, 1995). Natalense (1998) states that secretaries are taking on a professional entrepreneurial attitude, as they are creative, have initiative and are capable of making decisions, with practical and innovative ideas. In this sense, Garcia and D'Elia (2005) reinforce this assertion by pointing out that by merging technical and behavioral skills, which brings together "doing" and "advising", choosing tools that exercise relationship skills, communication, conflict management and monitoring objectives, the SE professional has expanded the dimension of their work.

In today's world, executive secretaries are required to have general knowledge and to manage processes in order to solve problems in a job market whose influence on an increasingly complex society does not allow them to invest in being just a clerk who solves simple day-to-day problems (BIANCHI; ALVARENGA; BIANCHI, 2003, p.3).

As such, the Executive Secretary must have specific academic training, work creatively, flexibly, have excellent communication and interpersonal skills, as well as provide quality advice to executives and be constantly updated, broadening their skills and their scope for inclusion in the job market.

According to Castelo (2007), the executive secretarial profession has undergone three major transformations that have given the profession and its practice new directions: the Age of Quality, the Age of Information Technology and the Age of Competence. These changes have given the professional a range of new responsibilities and the commitment to deliver visible results for the organization.

Garcia and D'Élia (2005) present a table comparing the profile of secretarial professionals.

Chart 4: Profile of the secretarial professional.

Yesterday	**Today**	**Future**

Dispersed training, self-taught.	Existence of specific training courses.	Professional maturity - code of ethics.
Lack of any requirement for upgrading	Refresher courses and special knowledge.	Constant improvement and development.
Lack of policy for recruitment and selection.	Requirement of qualifications and definition of duties and career plan.	Holistic vision and teamwork , professional awareness.
Bureaucratic organizations with isolated tasks.	Participative organizations, defined tasks, quality work, creativity and participation.	Entrepreneurial organizations, teamwork, global vision, flexible methodology, division of responsibility.
Secretariat function.	Secretarial work as a profession.	Secretary with professional recognition and committed to results.

Source: Garcia and D'Elia (2005, p. 25).

In their framework on the profile of the executive secretary, Garcia and D'elia (2005) assure that only a professional with a holistic vision, teamwork, maturity, among others, can satisfactorily meet the job market and its multiple demands. The authors present the characteristics that were required of this professional in the past as opposed to today's demands. "[...] the secretary is inserted into the management process of companies, as a vital professional, to work alongside the decision-making power, optimizing results in teams, projects, virtually and in the multiple options that the job market offers [...]" (GARCIA; D'ELIA, 2005, p.20). The skills developed by SE professionals are changing, given that the market is global. In this sense, Bianchi, Alvarenga and Bianchi (2003, p.7) add:

Nowadays, the trend in the job market is to demand generalized knowledge and multiple skills from professionals that transcend the borders of the country in which they live, and this demand is even greater when the focus is on professions such as secretarial work. The search for new technologies and skills, continuous learning, as well as partnership and a consequent spirit of cooperation are all characteristics that should not be lacking in this professional. The function of the secretary requires him to learn to analyze the market, define his mission, have objectives and recognize them in his work, have action plans and, of course, act ethically.

Castelo (2007) discusses these qualifications of the profile of the SE professional: advisor, manager, entrepreneur and consultant. As an advisor, the secretarial professional needs to have knowledge of the various business and administrative areas, thus carrying out communication and leadership practices. When it comes to acting as a manager, secretaries need to carry out their duties with quality and assertiveness, improving the optimization of results through planning, organizing and controlling activities. With regard to being an entrepreneur, this professional must be: active, creative, innovative, a negotiator, as well as other skills aimed at constant improvement in the various areas, implementing ideas that enhance the achievement of the company's objectives. And finally, the executive secretary as a consultant performs their function involved with the organization as a whole, making the necessary changes in order to achieve the company's and the executive's objectives.

According to Bianchi, Alvarenga and Bianchi (2003), as the fastest growing professional in the market, executive secretaries must remain attentive to the demands of the market and always be in tune with the standards of their field. Bond and Oliveira (2009, p.25) contribute: "with the changes that characterize the world scenario, professionals need to adapt to the market and, even more so, to the company in which they are working".

3 METHODOLOGY

3.1 Research Classification

With the general objective of the study being to verify the difficulties encountered by Executive Secretary professionals in the job market, this study used a qualitative approach, which according to Oliveira (2002) is research that can easily describe the complexity of a hypothesis or problem; to analyze the relationship between certain variables; to understand and classify dynamic processes experienced by social groups; to present contributions to the process of change and also the creation or shaping of a certain group's opinion, allowing a greater degree of depth and interpretation of the particularities of people's behaviors and attitudes. Therefore, the qualitative approach was the most appropriate for understanding the difficulties of entering the job market from the point of view of SE professionals.

It is also classified as exploratory research, since, according to Gil (2010), it is carried out with the aim of providing an approximate overview of a given fact in order to develop, clarify and modify concepts and ideas, with a view to formulating researchable problems for further study.

3.2 Delimitation of the Target Population and Sampling

With regard to the target population of this research project, it was centered on Executive Secretarial professionals in the city of Boa Vista (Roraima), as well as Human Resources (HR) managers. To this end, interviews were conducted with 12 ES professionals and 4 HR managers, using non-probabilistic convenience sampling, which according to Prodanov (2009, p. 109), "[...] the researcher selects the elements to which he has access". 23 contacts were made with SE professionals and 6 with HR managers, but only 12 professionals and 4 managers were obtained.

3.3 Data Collection Techniques

As for the collection technique, an in-depth interview was used, guided by a script of open questions. The in-depth interview, according to Roesch (2005), is a fundamental technique in qualitative research and is time-consuming and requires a lot of skill on the part of the interviewer. Its primary objective is to understand the meaning that the interviewees attribute to issues and situations in contexts that have not previously been structured based on the researcher's assumptions. The interviews were guided by a script of open questions (APPENDIX A) and grounded in theory. The first part of the script collected data on the socio-demographic profile of the interviewees, who were referred to as: SE professionals A to L; and HR managers 1 to 4.

3.4 Data Analysis Techniques

To process the data collected, we used content analysis, which, according to Roesch (2005), allows the researcher to understand and capture the perspective of the respondents, which is why the questions do not present a prior categorization of response alternatives. As the aim of this study is to capture individuals' understanding of the phenomenon of difficulties in entering the job market, this technique was the most appropriate.

4 PRESENTATION AND ANALYSIS OF DATA

4.1 Socio-demographic profile of the interviewees

Table 5 below describes the socio-demographic profile of executive secretarial professionals A to L.

Table 5: Distribution of the sociodemographic profile of secretarial professionals.

SOCIO-DEMOGRAPHIC PROFILE								
Interviewees	**Age**	**Gender**	**Company**	**Position**	**Time in office**	**Time in the job market**	**Income**	**Schooling**
A	21 a 30	F	Public	Executive Secretary	5 years	10 years	3 to 4 salaries s minim the	Doctorate
B	31 a 40	F	Public	Analyst Administrative/Executive Secretary	6 years	8 years	Above 8 minimum wages	Graduation
C	31 a 40	F	Public	Executive Secretary	1.5 years	21 years old	4 to 7 salaries s minim the	Postgraduate
D	31 a 40	F	Public	Secretary of the Committee on Family Rights, Women, Children, Adolescents and the Elderly and Social Action	4 years	10 years	4 to 7 salaries s minim the	Postgraduate
E	21 a 30	F	Private	Executive Secretary	1 year and 10 months	3 years and 10 months	3 to 4 salaries s minim	Postgraduate

							the	
F	21 a 30	M	Private	Administrative Assistant	3 years	3 years	3 to 4 salaries s minim the	Graduation
G	31 a 40	F	Public	Administration Assistant	6 months	1 year	3 to 4 salaries s minim the	Graduation
H	21 a 30	F	Public	Municipal Technician - Administrative Assistant	8 years	10 years	3 to 4 salaries s minimize	Graduation
I	21 a 30	F	Public	Executive Secretary	1 year and 9 months	3 years and 4 months	4 to 7 salaries s minim the	Postgraduate
J	21 a 30	F	Private	Executive Secretary	2 years	5 years	3 to 4 salaries s minimize	Graduation
K	31 a 40	F	Public	Executive Secretary	1 year	8 years	4 to 7 salaries s minimize	Graduation
L	31 a 40	F	Public	Executive Secretary	10 years	19 years old	4 to 7 salaries s minim the	Postgraduate

Source: Own elaboration.

The sample consisted of a group of 12 interviewees, classified in alphabetical order from A to L, 10 of whom work in the public sector and 2 in private companies. The data collected on the socio-demographic profile showed that 11 of the ES professionals are female and 1 is male. With regard to age, 6 interviewees were aged between 21 and 30 and the other 6 were aged between 31 and 40. In terms of job title, 9 of the interviewees work as Executive Secretaries and 3 as Administrative Assistants. It can be seen that 6 of the interviewees are graduates; 5 have postgraduate degrees and 1 has a doctorate. As for the Human Resources Managers, see table 6 below.

Chart 6: Distribution of the sociodemographic profile of the Human Resources Manager.

SOCIODEMOGRAPHIC PROFILE							
Interviewees	**Age**	**Gender**	**Type of company you work for**	**Time in office**	**Time in the job market**	**Income**	**Education**
A	Above 40	F	Public	11 years	25 years	4 to 7 minimum wages	Postgraduate
B	31 a 40	F	Public	10 years	20 years	4 to 7 minimum wages	Postgraduate
C	Above 40	F	Public	9 months	31 years old	4 to 7 minimum wages	Postgraduate
D	21 a 30	F	Private	6 years	8 years	4 to 7 minimum wages	Postgraduate

Source: Own elaboration.

Four Human Resources Managers were interviewed, and we chose to refer to them as HR Managers 1, 2, 3 and 4. All of them are female, three of whom work in public organizations and one in a private company. In terms of age, one of the interviewees is over 40, the other two are in the 21 to 30 age bracket and, finally, one is in the 31 to 40 age bracket. It was **noted** that the interviewees have been in the job market for a long time and that all of them have a postgraduate degree.

4.2 The Perception of Executive Secretarial Professionals on Competencies

As some authors have already pointed out in the theoretical discussion (MINARELI, 1995; BAGGIO et al., 2005; CHIAVENATO, 2002), competencies should be the main focus of each and every professional in order to get a good position in the job market. In this sense, questions 1, 2 and 3 of the interview script deal with the competencies that contribute to the organization's results.

The first question asked about the desired competencies. Interviewee A stated that the ES professional "needs to develop and demonstrate competencies [...], such as efficiency, effectiveness, exacerbated detachment from norms and procedures, flexibility, staying focused, aiming for results [...]" and added that the professional must have "the qualities inherent in any successful professional, such as respect, ethics, *know-how*, emotional intelligence, among others". Interviewee B said that an Executive Secretary "needs to be proactive, organized, outgoing and have a lot of self-discipline".

Interviewees C, D, G and I scored the following competencies: entrepreneurial, creative, delegating tasks, taking initiative, innovative, communication and also technical and human competencies. The interviewees' comments are in line with those made by Natalense (1998) and Garcia and D'Elia (2005), who point out that the professional assumes an entrepreneurial stance by being creative, taking the initiative and mixing technical and human skills to broaden their dimension.

However, there were some disagreements in the interviewees' answers about competencies such as: Communication, people management, interpersonal relationships, financial and calculation skills, knowledge of the law, good knowledge of Portuguese and text production, public service skills, time management, entrepreneurship (INTERVIEWEE E); Interpersonal Relations, Psychology, Ceremonial, Official Writing and Organization of Systems and Methods, Being up-to-date, a facilitator, innovative and resilient (INTERVIEWEE F); Agility, organization of the environment, planning, commitment to work, seeking to get the job done on time and well, manager, entrepreneur, advisor, efficiency and resourcefulness (INTERVIEWEE H); Proactivity, assertiveness, dexterity, time management and description, managing information, organized (INTERVIEWEE J); Having initiative in decision making, flexibility, creativity, knowing how to deal with the various situations of everyday life. (INTERVIEWEE K) and being a facilitator (INTERVIEWEE L). According to the data presented on competencies, it can be seen that proactivity and flexibility were the competencies most mentioned in the interviews

It can be concluded that when it comes to the competencies of the ES professional, the interviewees highlight the skills described above, and realize the importance of these competencies. The profile of an ES professional has a range of qualities that make for a healthy working environment and organizational climate; this set of skills makes for a better position in the job market.

4.3 Satisfaction and Recognition of the Secretarial Professional

In this item, the survey investigated[3] the satisfaction of SE professionals in their area of work and whether they are recognized in the market and in the organization. Interviewee A says she is satisfied with her work and, as far as recognition is concerned, she points out that she

3 Questions: 4, 5 and 6.

could be more highly valued. Note interviewee A's statement: "There is still a situation, like in Roraima, where you practically have no other field, apart from the public sector, which doesn't offer many vacancies for SE professionals, and the private sector is scarce". This also adds up to interviewee B, who says she is satisfied, although she points out that "[...] the problem is where we live, because the job market for executive secretaries here in Boa Vista is very restricted; we don't have private companies that value secretaries as professionals with higher education".

When interviewee C was asked about her satisfaction with her professional activity, it was clear that she was satisfied, but that there was a lack of recognition for secretarial professionals. On the other hand, interviewee D pointed out that she feels satisfied and recognized: "This professional has a global vision of the company and therefore maintains a productive relationship." Interviewee E added: "I feel valued because the secretarial professional is a fundamental part of the organization's success [...] many companies have a misunderstanding of the profession, they think that anyone can work as a secretary, and that's why there's no recognition."

Still in this context, interviewee F says that "His satisfaction is contributing to the institution, and that recognition is still low because we are part of a society that is unaware of the duties of the Executive Secretary professional". Interviewee G said: "I'm not satisfied because I don't work in the profession officially, and the Executive Secretary professional is not recognized, much less valued, especially in terms of salary [...] they don't know what they're doing [...]". This is in addition to interviewee J's statement: "I'm not satisfied and there isn't much recognition of the secretarial professional in Boa Vista, because they think that the stereotype of this professional is just to answer phone calls, take messages and serve coffee [...] whereas this professional is a fundamental part of any organization." Interviewee K adds: "I don't feel satisfied and there's no recognition in many places because they think of the professional merely as a secretary [...] and they still don't know what the SE professional really does in the job market".

Interviewee H says that for her "satisfaction to be complete, only when she is working as an Executive Secretary". She adds, "Recognition still leaves something to be desired, and I believe that we as secretarial professionals and academics should publicize the profession more, as there are still many managers who don't know the profile of the ES professional."

Still on the subject of satisfaction, interviewee I points out that she is satisfied "and that recognition is growing more and more in the state of Roraima, where the market revolves around the public service, and there are more and more vacancies for the position of Executive Secretary. Interviewee L points out that "I'm satisfied because I love what I do [...]", she tries to keep up to date and, in terms of recognition, it's worth noting that there is a barrier between the secretary who used to dedicate herself only to looking after the diary, answering phone calls and writing letters dictated by her boss. Nowadays, they have a much more strategic role, acting as advisors and need to be better prepared to carry out their duties with a more executive attitude.

According to the interviewees, 7 are satisfied but don't feel recognized, 2 are satisfied and feel recognized and 3 are dissatisfied. Many of the respondents say that they see ES professionals as mere secretaries, without any kind of training, without any range of activities, and that many organizations still don't recognize Executive Secretaries. The interviewees who are satisfied and recognized point out that recognition is growing all the time.

4.4 Difficulties in entering the job market

In questions 7, 8, 9 and 10, the interviewees gave their opinions on the difficulties in the job market and the aspects that were not developed during their degree. When asked about the difficulties encountered in entering the job market, the following was obtained: Interviewee A stated that "I didn't have any difficulties, when I graduated, a public examination came up, which I applied for, dedicated myself to studying and was approved in first place" But she added that "There are difficulties due to the lack of vacancies for the position of Executive Secretary [...] due to the scarcity of the private sector in the market in Roraima".

And interviewee B pointed out that "The state of Roraima only has public tenders that *offer* opportunities to work as executive secretaries, and that private companies don't have a decent salary for secretarial graduates and there is no recognition for this professional". Interviewee C observes that "Managers don't recognize this professional, so it's difficult to make them understand that there's a big difference in having a trained professional, not a secretary by appointment, but someone who can really make a difference within the company, but I didn't have any difficulties, I graduated and passed the exam, in six months I was already working" As can be seen in interviewee D's statement "I didn't have any difficulties, I was already working in the area". And interviewee K said: "I didn't have any difficulties, it wasn't hard to get into the job market, but the market is very demanding".

Interviewee E replied: "I found it difficult, because generally for this position, as it is a position of trust, you need an appointment as well as competence". Interviewee F points out that "It was difficult at first because of society's lack of knowledge about the duties of a secretarial professional". Interviewee G goes on to say that "In the private sector, it's still difficult because there's no appreciation of the executive secretarial profession, but in the public sector it's easy because there's already a public competition for the position of executive secretary, so you don't encounter many difficulties". Interviewee H added: "My difficulty was the fear of moving forward, but over time you realize that things are possible and that in fact [...] we have difficulties." As interviewee I adds, "I found it difficult in the face of strong competition in the job market".

And, from interviewee J's perspective, "Yes, it was difficult, because there are few vacancies for graduate secretaries, and when they do come up there is a lot of competition for them, where the winner is the person who has the most work experience, due to the fact that they graduated a long time ago". And interviewee L: "As I was already working before I finished my degree, and I was already working as an administrative assistant, it was just a step, I didn't have much difficulty".

As a result, it can be seen that 6 of the executive secretarial professionals interviewed had no difficulties in finding a job in the market for which they were trained, while the other 6 had difficulties in finding a job in an organization. ES professionals face challenges in terms of salaries, as some of those interviewed feel that they are not commensurate with their duties, a lack of vacancies, mainly in the private sector, strong competition in the job market and a lack of appreciation for the profession.

And with regard to question 8, which deals with the aspects that were not developed satisfactorily during her degree and what they could have done to help her enter the job market, interviewee A pointed out that "Today, as a professional, I realize that I lacked better development in some subjects during the course, but I learned to be self-taught [...] if I could say this to students, seek knowledge, and even more so, if you're taking a course satisfactorily [...] certainly, if you do that, be resourceful [...].If I could say this to students, they should seek knowledge, and even more so, even if they are studying a subject satisfactorily [...] surely, if students do this, are resourceful, and have absorbed the knowledge learned in the classroom and outside it well, they shouldn't encounter too many difficulties in the job market, and in fact, these are the ones who get the job". Interviewee B, on the other hand, said: "Yes, there was a lack, first of all the archivology subject left something to be desired [...] there was a lack of a subject focused on interpersonal relationships, there was no contact with the public [...] there was a lack of practice, there was only theory, [...] there was a lack of action, I don't know if a little more from the university, to show companies the competences of higher level secretaries".

In this perspective, interviewee C adds, "Yes, there were many, especially for analytical and critical thinking [...] I didn't learn anything in English and the little bit of Spanish, as I don't develop it, ends up not being incorporated into the profession." And interviewee E says, "Yes, there was a deficiency in the teaching of languages, English and Spanish, which prevented me from being able to apply for vacancies in multinational companies, whose requirement is fluency in the languages mentioned." And interviewee F says, "Yes, there should have been more classes in photoshop and coreldraw to acquire more adaptability to technology. Interviewee F "Yes, there should have been more classes in photoshop and coreldraw so that we could become more adapted to technology". Interviewee G said: "Yes, the IT area and the language area weren't very good.

very well developed". Interviewee K said: "Yes, the difficulty was mainly in the ceremonial subject. The university lacked a greater commitment to theory and practice".

For interviewee D "No, for me, they were developed satisfactorily". This is in addition to interviewee H's statement: "Yes, all the subjects give us some kind of knowledge, where some can be applied in the market and others cannot. When I was an undergraduate, one of the most important subjects was methodology, but it wasn't well developed with the class". Interviewee I added: "No, because the course has a good theoretical basis, which is essential for entering the civil service. The factors that could be better developed in the course are more necessary in the professional's work, where practice is required." Still in this context, interviewee J corroborates "I believe that the course is very good and depends a lot on the student, for example in the area of languages, you can't just rely on the knowledge acquired at the institution, you need to take a separate course to be able to perform better, and in relation to the events, there could be more simulated hypothetical situations for students to understand and practice". Finally, interviewee L points out that she doesn't see the course in a comprehensive way.

In the perception of SE professionals, it was noted that some of the interviewees lacked certain aspects in their undergraduate studies that were not developed satisfactorily, such as: language subjects, computer skills, methodology and other aspects that could have helped them in the job market; as a result, there is sometimes a certain difficulty on the part of the students, which implies a lack of characteristics that should be developed by professionals, such as: being action-oriented and making things happen, as well as having personal initiative (BAGGIO et al., 2005; CHIAVENATO, 2002). This will ensure that professionals are always up-to-date and seeking new knowledge in order to adapt to the competitive market.

When asked about the challenges and difficulties faced by secretarial professionals, what universities could do to minimize the differences required, the interviewees noted:

Chart 7: SE professionals' perceptions of educational institutions

Interviewees	**Answers**
A	"Firstly, the hiring of teachers dedicated to the professional training of ES, which would not lead to a deficit in the training of some students. In order to keep things moving in this healthy direction, students should evaluate the teaching staff, so that the course board can see what is lacking, what is good and could be improved, in short, to correct the

	problems and get better and better. Continued training for students is also essential, with *workshops*, scientific-academic events, junior companies, paid internships - which would allow practical teaching as well as a stipend for students, and other policies that should be evaluated in each educational institution together with institutions that support the profession, such as trade unions, and institutions that will hire these professionals. I believe that the ideal thing is for these institutions to talk to each other, so that they can find the best way forward for everyone" (*sic*).
B	"More partnerships with companies to show what they are putting on the job market, that it's not just a technician, people with higher education are coming out, people with the skills to be able to manage, advise, do this work in line with the education level, know what a graduate is and what a technician is, make this contact with companies to give them a closer view of the SE professional and their skills" (*sic*).
C	"[...] The University should publicize the professions, so that organizations get to know these professionals, as well as interacting with the job market, but perhaps it's the students who should be doing this, with CBT work and fairs, or something similar, together with the University, as well as more projects, such as PIBID, with organizations, teachers committed to the course."
D	"Creating different training and skills for each area of the professional's knowledge, enabling greater career diversity."
E	"Worrying about hiring qualified teachers to teach all the subjects, because they are all important and sooner or later you will always need to use the knowledge acquired in the classroom."
F	"The Federal University of Roraima has been fulfilling its duties, but what we lack is union representation, because it has disappeared from local society. This puts us at a certain disadvantage compared to the regional councils, which are organized, such as CRM, CRC, CRA, CREA

	and others that have their councils active to claim their rights representing a class. FENASSEC - the Federation of Secretaries - has been fighting for the establishment of a Professional Council for Secretaries, which involves a lot of politics".
G	"It's evolving, the course specifically is flowing, before there were no Masters, Doctors [...] and today the Executive Secretariat course is well attended."
H	"I believe that Federal Universities should invest more in policies to value professionals, one idea would be to send or create a program
	to send the profile of the secretarial students to the companies that hire them, so that they can recognize the profession".
I	"Better linking theory and practice, because when you enter the job market, the practice factor is highly demanded, but little explored in the course."
J	"To have more dynamic classes, where learning is better utilized, and as it is an area that deals a lot with people, there would need to be more practical classes in order to put into practice everything that is learned in theory."
K	"The university could do more to publicize the profile of the secretarial professional, because not everyone really knows who this professional is. Not just publicize it, but also try to do this in the companies where the students do their internships, showing what that professional can do for the company and also giving them an opportunity later on to show their work and contribute to the company."
L	"It's just recognition, even on the part of the big companies, and the job market, considering that the universities are injecting qualified professionals."

Source: Own elaboration.

In relation to the answers cited by the interviewees in chart 7, it can be seen that the Executive

Secretarial professionals indicate that educational institutions should invest more in hiring professors dedicated to teaching this professional; that they should have more partnerships with companies to show the profile and skills that the ES professional has, so that everyone knows about this professional, and thus foster the appreciation and recognition of this profession in the job market.

4.5 Profile and Competencies of the SE Professional in the Perception of HR Managers.

Questions 1, 2, 3 and 4 deal with the skills and profile required by companies in the job market for executive secretaries. According to interviewee 1, the skills required of secretarial professionals focus on: "advising, managing information, preparing documents, coordinating and controlling teams and activities, controlling correspondence and organizing events and trips [...] and this profile follows the rules proposed by the MEC".

According to Interviewee 2, "The secretarial professional must have perfection and excellence in everything they do and in the way they express themselves, interest and responsibility [...]". Interviewees 3 and 4 explain that the profile of an ES professional must firstly "have a degree in Executive Secretarial, as well as being able to send out documents, know about filing and writing, as well as secretarial meetings, playing the role of an Administrative Assistant".

With regard to question 2, relating to the appropriate profile of the SE professional desired in the market, interviewees 1, 2, 3 and 4 responded as follows:

Chart 8: Profile of the secretarial professional as perceived by HR managers.

Interviewees	Answers
1	"A professional who is proactive, responsible, communicative, creative, interpersonal in addition to technical and human skills."

2	"[...] It is essential that this professional seeks new visions of the world, self-knowledge and is able to constantly value himself, be proactive, flexible and adapt to changes so that he is able to win in the competitive market [...]".
3	"That this professional has proactivity, agility, communication skills and fluency in Spanish."
4	"[...] problem-solving, having an attitude, being proactive and flexible."

Source: Own elaboration.

In relation to the answers above, it can be seen that the opinions differed in some respects, but they all agree that secretarial professionals have to be proactive.

When asked about the differences between the graduate profile and the profile the market wants, and what can be done to minimize this difference. Interviewee 1 explains that "there are differences because before they appointed an SE professional [...] as an Administrative Assistant and there was a certain limitation [...]; to minimize this difference is to make very good use of the SE professional in the body, which was not the case before, and they perform their duties very well, meeting the requirements assigned by the manager".

Interview 2 emphasizes:

Yes, the profile when graduating is completely different, taking into account the discrimination of the professional in the job market, in the future the professional will be the one who will work for the company and in a team, take moderate risks and invest, will be motivated by goals and objectives to be achieved, maximize the use of resources, obtaining results as well as being responsible for managing people, managing information and documents, above all, will be an entrepreneur. [...] professionals need to possess these characteristics in order to be successful.

Interviewee 3 said that "Not that the market doesn't demand it, but executive secretaries offer many good skills, but they don't give them the opportunity to exploit their abilities". Interviewee 4 corroborates this: "Some ES professionals don't have fluency in a second language and are often shy, which hinders the communication process and what I would do to minimize these differences: language courses [...] and psychological support."

It can be seen that some Human Resources managers value the Executive Secretary profession highly, as they have full confidence in the performance of their skills, and know that they are capable of solving problems that may arise, which is very important to organizations.

4.6 Job placement

Question 5 asked about the chances of an ES professional getting a good position in the job market. Interviewee 1 pointed out that "the institution does a talent map and checks the capacity of the ES professional [...]" and added, "those who aren't seen aren't remembered, no matter how good a professional they are".

Interviewee 2 adds: "To be a good professional, it's not enough to have great computer skills, to manage contacts, agendas and/or services; to be successful, professionals need to keep themselves informed and have knowledge not only about their work, but also about the company; only with these characteristics will the SE professional be respected and valued."

According to interviewee 3, "There is no job plan that covers the Executive Secretary, because he plays the role of administrative assistant within the institution [...] there is a public competition". Interviewee 4 pointed out that "The chances are good since entry is by public examination".

Thus, it can be seen from the interviews that the managers stress that this professional has to have the ability and possess some desirable characteristics (proactive, flexible, facilitator, multifunctional, multi-skilled, among others) in order to be recognized in the organization and add to this the fact, according to two managers, that placement on the job market is by public examination.

4.7 Opportunities and Challenges for the SE Professional

When asked about the opportunities and challenges for this professional to keep up with changes in the market, the following answers were obtained: Interviewee 1 pointed out that this professional "must study and qualify as well as doing their job, they have to keep up with the profile, following the dynamics of the job market".

According to interviewee 2:

The new business environment has changed the profile of the secretarial professional, who has begun to play a prominent role in the company, his potential has been recognized, creating the possibility of building a career as promising as that of any other executive. The transformation in secretarial functions didn't happen by chance; it went hand in hand with the opening up of markets, the re-engineering of companies and the need for multidisciplinary professionals with decision-making powers within corporations.

Interviewee 3 answered as follows: "This professional needs to dedicate themselves to knowing the work they are going to do and must always use common sense and balance so that they can transmit confidence and the ability to solve problems, remaining open to new learning when carrying out the activities entrusted to them, always keeping up to date, as this will enable them to succeed in keeping up with changes in the market". And interviewee 4 points out that "it is necessary to always be studying and updating your knowledge, as well as helping to stand out in your markets".

Therefore, the managers' perception of the opportunities and challenges showed that the opportunities are wide-ranging, although there are still obstacles to be overcome. It is worth emphasizing the need for executive secretaries to keep up to date, seeking new knowledge and qualifications so that they can keep up with changes in the market.

4.8 The importance of the secretarial professional in the job market

When asked about the degree of importance of the SE professional for managers in organizations?

Interviewee 1 highlights:

This professional has a degree of excellence [...] and that makes a huge difference; [...] in addition to being versatile and multifunctional, characteristics that are of fundamental importance in the globalized world to which we belong and that make a big difference in the professional profile, which will have a lot of space and recognition to conquer.

Interviewee 2 points out that "today's secretarial professional is much more important and has more complex tasks in a position of trust within any company, being a 'right-hand man' for the executive [...]". Interviewee 2 also points out that the secretarial professional takes on the role of advisor, helping to achieve the organization's objectives and assisting in decision-making.

Interviewee 3 points out that "In addition to the frequent changes in the job market, secretaries are very important because not every manager has the skills that an ES professional has, such as: knowing how to impose themselves, expressing themselves, contributing to the organization in a facilitating way". And interviewee 4 corroborates this: "It's extremely important, since it's this professional who makes it possible for organizations to function".

Based on the interviews, it was found that executive secretaries are fundamental to the organization due to the flexibility of their skills and attributions. They are professionals who are able to identify problems and solve them, facilitating the achievement of the organization's objectives, but in order to do so they must constantly qualify and improve their knowledge.

FINAL CONSIDERATIONS

As a result of the high level of competition, ES professionals have to keep up with the changes in order to adapt their profile to the demands of the job market, which will be another determining factor for their insertion and permanence in the world of work. In this context, this study set out to verify the difficulties encountered by executive secretarial professionals in entering the job market.

Based on the results of the survey, it can be said that the difficulties faced by executive secretaries in entering the job market are: the lack of vacancies for executive secretaries in public tenders, the scarcity of vacancies in the private sector in Roraima; remuneration not commensurate with the profession; lack of recognition from managers; lack of knowledge of their duties and a demanding, competitive market.

In addition, when asked about the difficulties of entering the market, the perception of SE professionals was that some of the interviewees did not experience any difficulties and still feel recognized and satisfied. However, a significant proportion of those interviewed found it difficult to enter the world of work and still don't feel recognized, let alone satisfied.

With regard to the limitations of the research, since it is qualitative, the data cannot be taken as conclusive, nor can generalizations be inferred. Based on the results found, it can be seen that this research has contributed to enriching the field of Executive Secretaries, through the perception of ES professionals and HR managers on the following subjects: difficulties in entering the job market, satisfaction, recognition, importance, profile and competencies of this professional, as well as in the sense of encouraging studies in the job market, knowing the professional competencies.

In this sense, it is recommended that future studies involving a quantitative approach be carried out on the population of graduates of the Executive Secretarial course, in order to find out their perspectives regarding their insertion in the job market, as well as carrying out research that aims to assess the congruence between the professional profile outlined in the Pedagogical Project of the course - PPC and the expectations of the market.

REFERENCES

ARRUDA, Adriano. **Labor Market.** 2010. Available at: <http://www.artigonal.com/carreira-artigos/adriano-arruda-mercado-de-trabalho-1722942.html.> Accessed on: 05/06/2013.

BAGGIO, Leticia et al. 2005. **How to maintain employability in times of crisis**. Available at: <http://www.fsh.edu.br/revista/artigo1-como-manter-empregabilidade.pdf.> Accessed on: 12/06/2013.

BERTAN, Simone Teixeira. The employability of executive secretaries graduating from UNESC - Classes 2008 and 2009. Final paper for the Executive Secretarial course. Universidade do Extremo Sul Catarinense - UNESC. Criciùma, 2010.

BERTOLINO, Valdessara. **The multifunctional professional.** Published on: September 21, 2002. Available at:< http://www.secretariando.com.br/carreira/carr-30.htm.> Accessed on: 12/06/2013.

BIANCHI, Anna Cecilia de Moraes; ALVARENGA, Marina; BIANCHI, Roberto. **Orientation for secretarial internships**: papers, projects and monographs.Sao Paulo: Pioneira Thomson Learning, 2003.

BOND, Maria Thereza; OLIVEIRA, Marlene de**. Manual do profissional** de **secretariado,** v3: secretario como cogestor. Curitiba: Ibpex, 2009. Available: <http:// books.google.com.br>, accessed on: 22/10/2013.

CARVALHO, Antonio Pires de; GRISSON, Diller (Org.). **Manual do secretariado executivo**. Sao Paulo: D"Livros, 2002.

CASTELO; Marcia Janaina. **Academic Training and the Professional Performance of**

Executive Secretary. (2007) - Available at <http://www.fenassec.com.br/consec_3lugar.pdf> accessed on: 02/10/2013.

CHIAVENATO, Idalberto. **Career and competence**: managing your greatest capital. Sao Paulo: Saraiva, 2002.

D'ELIA, Maria Elizabete. **Professionalism: you** can't not have it. Sao Paulo: Editora Gente, 1997.

DIAS, Jezilda Gomes Fernandes. et al. **GPT - Gestao de pessoas e Relaçôes de Trabalho.O papel e a valorizaçao da secretà executiva no mundo corporativo.** XXIV. ENANGRAD. FLORIANÓPOLIS, 2013.

FACHINI, Mauricio Vitório. **A New Job Market for a New Professional.** Feb. 2009 - Available at:< http://www.artigonal.com/carreira-artigos/novo-mercado-de-trabalhoopara-um-novo-profissional-792001.html.> Accessed on: 12/07/2013.

FLEURY, Maria, Tereza Leme; SARSUR, Amyra, Moyzes. Nenhum a menos: desvendando conceitos sobre gestao por competências in: Administraçao com arte: experiências vividas de ensino-aprendizagem. Org: Eduardo Davel, Sylvia Constant Vergara and djahanchah Philip Ghadiri. Sao Paulo: Atlas, 2007.

GARCIA, Edméa; D'ELIA, Maria Elizabete Silva. **Executive Secretary**. Sao Paulo: IOB Thomson, 2005.

GIL, Antonio Carlos. **Method and Techniques of Social Research.** Sao Paulo: Atlas, 2010.

HILSDORF, Carlos. **What is Employability?** 2008. Available at: <http://www.administradores.com.br/informe-se/artigos/o-que-e-empregabilidade/31256/> Accessed on: 13/07/2013.

LAKATOS, Eva Maria. **Scientific Methodology.** Sao Paulo: Atlas, 2010.

MALHOTRA, Naresh K. **Marketing Research**: An Applied Orientation. Porto Alegre: Bookman, 2012.

MAXIMIANO, Antonio Cesar Amaru. **Teoriageraldaadministraçâo**: da revoluçao urbana à revoluçao digital. Sao Paulo: Atlas, 2004.

MINARELLI, José Augusto. **Employability:** The path of stones. Sao Paulo: Editora Gente, 1995.

NASCIMENTO, Arielly. et al .2005. **Career and Employability in the Secretarial Area.** Available at:<http://erevista.unioste.br/index.php/expectativa/article/view/408> accessed on:13/07/2013

NATALENSE, Liana. **The secretary of the future**. Sao Paulo: Qualitymark, 1998.

OLIVEIRA, Silvio Luiz de,**Tratado** de **Metodologia Cientifica:** research projects, TGI, TCC, monographs, dissertations and theses. Sao Paulo: Pioneira Thomson Learning, 2002.

PORTER, Michael. **Competitive Advantage**: creating and sustaining superior performance. Rio de Janeiro: Elsevier, 1989-35ª Reprint.

PERES, Angelo**. The World of Work and Employability**. 2005. Available at: <http://internativa.com.br/artigo_rh_06.html> Accessed on: 13/07/2013.

PRODANOV, CLEBER CRISTIANO. **Methodology of Scientific Work**: methods and techniques of research and academic work. Novo Hamburgo: FEEVALE, 2009.

ROESCH, Sylvia Maria Azevedo. **Internship and research projects in administration: a** guide for internships, term papers, dissertations and case studies. Sao Paulo: Atlas, 2005.

ROSA, Jaqueline Silva. The dynamics of collective competences in cooperation networks.

Master's thesis (Postgraduate Program in Administration). University of Vale do Rio dos Sinos- UNISINOS. Sao Leopoldo (RS), 2007.

SAVIANI, José Roberto. **Entrepreneurship**: how companies should act to keep people with a high employability rate on their staff. Sao Paulo: Makron Books, 1997.

VEIGA, Denise Rachel. **Secretarial Guide:** Behavioral Techniques. Sao Paulo: Érica, 2007

APPENDIX

The aim of this research is to verify the difficulties encountered by executive secretarial professionals in finding a place in the Boa Vista job market. It is the conclusion of the course work of Antonia Aline Rodrigues, a student on the executive secretarial course at UFRR.

Interview script

Respondent: Executive Secretary.

I - Identification of the interviewee

Age:EZI 21 to 30 years □31 to 40 years □ over 40 years

Gender:□ female □ male

Type of company: □ public □ private

Function or position:

Time in office:

Time in the job market:

Income: □ from 3 to 4 minimum wages □ from 4 to 7 minimum wages □ above 8 minimum wages

Education: Postgraduate □ Master's □ Doctorate □ Other

I - Questions

1. What competencies are desirable for the SE professional to contribute to managing the organization's results?
2. What is the relationship between your current work and your professional training?
3. What competence(s) do you think are fundamental in the profile of the secretarial

professional Executive?

4. How satisfied are you with your current professional activity?

5. What do you think of the professional recognition of SE in the job market?

6. Do you feel recognized in your company? Explain yourself?

7. What difficulties have you encountered in entering the job market?

8. In your opinion, do you think that there were aspects of your degree that were not developed satisfactorily during the course and that could have helped you to enter the job market? Yes/no. Which aspects?

9. How long after graduating did you look for a job?

10. Faced with the challenges and difficulties faced by SE professionals, what can universities do to minimize the differences required?

Interview script

Respondent: Human Resources Manager - HR

I - Identification of the interviewee

Age:EZI 21 to 30 years □31 to 40 years □ over 40 years

Sex: □ female □ male

Type of company:□ public □ private

Time in office:

Time in the job market:

Income: □ from 3 to 4 minimum wages □ from 4 to 7 minimum wages □ above 8 minimum wages

Education: Postgraduate □ Master's □ Doctorate □ Other

I - Questions

1. What skills does your company require for the profile of the SE position?

2. What is the appropriate profile of the SE professional that managers are looking for in the job market in Boa Vista?

3. Do you see any differences between the profile of the SE graduate and the profile required in the job market? If so, which ones?

4. What do you recommend to minimize this difference?

5. What are the chances of an Executive Secretary who is just starting out in this company getting a good position?

6. In your opinion, what are the opportunities and challenges for SE professionals to keep up with the changes in the globalized world and succeed in their careers?

7. How important are executive secretaries to managers in organizations?

Printed by Books on Demand GmbH, Norderstedt / Germany